ZINGERS
FOR 1ST-3RD GRADERS

12 REAL-LIFE
CHARACTER BUILDERS

David and Kathy Lynn

ZondervanPublishingHouse
Grand Rapids, Michigan
A Division of HarperCollinsPublishers

Zingers for 1st-3rd Graders
Copyright © 1993 by David and Kathy Lynn

Requests for information should be addressed to:
Zondervan Publishing House
Grand Rapids, Michigan 49530

ISBN 0-310-37221-6

Edited by Rose Pruiksma
Interior design by Jamison • Bell Advertising & Design
Cover design by Terry Dugan Design
Illustrations by Corbin Hillam

Printed in the United States of America

93 94 95 96 97 /DP/ 10 9 8 7 6 5 4 3 2 1

CONTENTS

MORE TOPICS:

THE FOLLOWING ADDITIONAL TOPICS
CAN BE FOUND IN VOLUME TWO,

MORE ZINGERS:

Advertising

Effects of Competition

Drug Use

Being Made Fun Of

TV Violence

Nicotine Use

Bad Influence of Friends

Obeying Parents

Good Friend Moving

Dealing With the News

Childhood Stress

Being Bullied

INTRODUCTION

In recent visits to elementary schools we have seen dramatic changes in children's behavior and attitudes. We have observed kids dressed in mini-skirts, wearing nylons, sporting high heels, and overloaded with makeup. And those are just the boys—you should see the girls! It's a joke, of course, but sometimes the joke is close to reality. Kids are growing up fast. Children in the lower elementary grades now face issues that were reserved for yesterday's adolescents. These issues include choice of videos to rent, intense pressure from sports competition, vulgar language, dealing with the news, and TV violence.

The Growing-Up-Too-Fast Syndrome

David Elkind—a developmental psychologist—and other writers have pointed out that children today face enormous pressure to rush through childhood. Younger and younger children are forced prematurely into the world of adulthood. Their childhood years are no longer a guaranteed sanctuary from the pressures and stress of adult life. Talk with elementary school teachers and you may be surprised to hear them discuss childhood stress. The pressures to succeed, the increased competition from organized sports at younger ages, and the uncertainty of family life all are producing symptoms of stress in our children. Stress signs in children such as headaches, teeth-grinding, out-of-the-ordinary crying, upset stomachs, and nervous behaviors are commonly reported by elementary school teachers.

There are other signs that children are pressured into growing up too quickly. Look at the dress of children and you will not see much difference between the way children, teenagers, and adults dress. Children are getting hip, teenage-oriented haircuts. The next time you are at the video rental store, observe the kinds of movies kids are picking out for their parents to rent. Or simply talk to kids about what they discuss and do on the elementary playground and you will find them knowing and talking more about divorce, violence, boy/girl relationships, and abuse than previous generations.

This rush to grow up has blurred the distinction between what it means to be a child, an adolescent, and an adult. The growing-up-too-fast syndrome has produced an "experimenting-too-soon" phenomenon whereby children during their elementary school years now engage in behaviors normally associated with older children and teenagers.

The diagram to the right illustrates what we think is happening with today's young people.

Children's behavior, until about age nine, differs little from the values they have been taught. But the seventh

AGE	VALUES	BEHAVIORS
1–8	Minimal Departure	
9–13	Moderate Departure	
14–18	Maximum Departure	
19–24	Moderate Departure	
25+	Minimal Departure	

year of life marks a dramatic change. Between the ages of seven and ten, children become more capable of taking other points of view. They begin losing their innocence as they learn more about the world and its cruelty. With their increasing ability to see other viewpoints, they also begin to consider the values they have been taught and discover the plethora of behavioral choices available to them. Most kids, no matter how protected, now realize that other kids make choices that they never knew were available or that they had been taught were wrong. This is why Zinger discussions with seven- to ten-year-olds are vital. Kids need to talk about the available choices with adults who can positively influence those choices. Zinger discussions can and should be directed toward helping kids process their confusion regarding many of these choices.

Even though children between the ages of seven and ten don't experiment with as many behaviors inconsistent with their learned values as do preadolescents and adolescents, they do face behavioral choices because of the barrage of pressures pushing them to do things like watch movies with inappropriate content, use vulgar language, or make fun of others. We have chosen to call these choices "pressure points" because they pressure our kids to make immediate decisions of right and wrong without the help and support of societal standards.

During the preadolescent years, young people begin to experiment with behaviors that conflict with their values. (We are grateful to the late Hershel Thornburg, a former professor, for his insights into the values-behavior inconsistency problem in young people.) This experimenting-too-soon phenomenon begins so early because there are so many more opportunities to experiment in today's world. Past generations of American youths were presented with a Judeo-Christian moral standard that prevailed throughout society. The home was supported by the church, school, media, and neighborhood in presenting an agreed-upon set of moral standards and behaviors to kids. Today, preadolescents are exposed to a smorgasbord of choices. (If you are also working with preadolescent young people you may want to use the *Zingers* and *More Zingers* written for 9-12 year olds.)

By adolescence these pressure points have reached their peak, creating a maximum departure between behaviors and values. However, during the career/college years of nineteen to twenty-four, there is less discrepancy between young peoples' values and behaviors. They begin to return to the values taught them by the home and church. By adulthood, most people have returned to their childhood values. This explanation of values and behaviors supports the biblical model of Proverbs 22:6: "Train a child in the way he should go, and when he is old he will not turn from it."

Here we are concerned with the childhood and early preadolescent years from seven to ten, when kids begin to experiment with behaviors inconsistent with the values they have been taught. Research appears to indicate that the greater the inconsistency between values and behaviors, the more likely it is that the young person's values will change to conform with the new behaviors. Zingers give you the opportunity within a Christian context to positively influence the values of young people as well as their behavioral choices.

BENEFITS OF A ZINGER DISCUSSION

You and your group will experience a great many benefits by using Zingers as part of your Christian education. Take a look at the following benefits to see if these are things you want for your group.

1. Zinger discussions diffuse the pressure points of the growing-up experience. We must become more intentional in teaching our values to young people so they have a foundation from which to operate when they confront pressure points. In the past, it was not necessary to teach values regularly and actively because they were demonstrated and reinforced by society's Judeo-Christian standards. But with the breakdown of Judeo-Christian values has come an increasing number of values choices and, consequently, more demanding pressure points.

Zinger discussions are one method of intentionally passing along our Christian values. Zingers focus on specific issues, providing you with opportunities to openly discuss specific Christian values and behaviors. You can talk directly about the pressure points facing the children in your group.

2. Zinger discussions transfer learning to the real world. The four walls of the church, school, or club provide an artificial world for Christian kids. As young people move from grade to grade within their Christian education, they often find that what they learn is not related to real-life experiences. When truths learned at church, school, or club do not work in the real world, kids will more readily question and throw out their faith when they are with their friends. What young people need is a Christian education that is relevant to their life experiences.

Kids can best transfer their learning to the real world if group discussions in the classroom setting closely approximate real-life situations, feelings, and issues. When children encounter similar situations, feelings, or issues in their world, they can then more easily transfer the knowledge and skills they acquired in the classroom setting. The closer the discussions are to true-to-life situations, the more easily the transfer will occur. Zingers have been designed to facilitate this kind of transfer. Based upon real-life stories, Zingers take your kids' world and bring it into the classroom for examination. As a group you can then learn to apply God's Word to the realities of their world.

3. Zinger discussions provide a valuable child/adult learning partnership opportunity. We often see children as recipients of our adult knowledge. We believe that we know what is best for the children and view our young people as objects or recipients without much to offer. We dominate discussions and other Christian educational experiences with our right answers and spiritual insights. We are like the disciples who shooed the children away from Jesus (Luke 18:15-17). If we see kids only as recipients of our spiritual insights, our dialogues with them will quickly become monologues. We will wonder why our young people refuse to "open up" with us. The problem is with us. Our view of children has become distorted by our "adultness." What can we do? We need to see children as resources of wisdom and spiritual insight.

Zinger discussions offer an adult leader the opportunity to create a child/adult learning partnership. You can do this by:

a. Actively listening to your group members as they tell their stories related to the Zinger situation.

b. Respecting the opinions of all your group members regardless of how off-base any of their comments are.

c. Empathizing with your young people about what it means to be a child in today's world. You can do this by remembering what it was like to be young yourself.

d. Spending time with children. Most of your kids spend the majority of their time with their peers whether in large classrooms, after-school programs, or organized sports programs. A Zinger discussion allows adults to be actively involved in children's lives. Spending time dialoguing with kids about important issues will earn you the right to be heard by them.

4. Zinger discussions provide you with a spiritual gauge of your group.
Zinger discussions will help you discover what the kids in your group believe and how they are acting upon their beliefs. This is invaluable for the young people's worker who wishes to understand children's needs.

Zinger discussions will also help your kids discover what they believe. Zingers provide you with the opportunity to engage your kids in dialogue about their beliefs and the inconsistency between their beliefs, actions, and God's Word.

5. Zinger discussions encourage positive peer pressure. A guided Zinger discussion gets kids talking with adults and each other and gives them the chance to lead and influence each other in positive directions. To counter the effects of negative peer pressure, use Zingers to create pressure to do what is honoring to God. Your group members can encourage positive behavior and values in one another.

INGREDIENTS FOR A GOOD ZINGER DISCUSSION

You may be asking yourself why we are recommending a Zinger discussion rather than a Zinger lecture or a Zinger sermon. Why not just read the Zinger and tell the group what they should and should not do?

Research has found that adults possess a valuable tool in helping young people learn right from wrong. That tool is dialogue. Zingers allow you to dialogue with the children in your group through a discussion. But good discussions don't just happen—we make them happen. To help your group enter into a meaningful, life-changing discussion, you must pay attention to the four ingredients of a good discussion: correct attitude, healthy ground rules, discussion motivators, and perceptive questioning.

Attitude Check

If you believe adults know what is best for kids, then you will have difficulty leading a good Zinger discussion. Why? Because adults do not always know what is best, and kids know it. If adults did know what was best for kids, youth culture would not be in the mess it is today! Viewing children as the recipients of our good intentions and valuable knowledge only sets us up to be tested by kids. Young people are not stupid. They will see through our patronizing attitudes. What young people need is a child/adult partnership that communicates acceptance and respect. Your group members need to know that their contributions to any discussion are important. Each child's opinion is worth hearing and considering. This does not mean every opinion is worth accepting. Affirmation and approval are two very different things. For a good discussion to occur, however, your group members will need to know that whatever they say will not be laughed at, put down, or considered stupid.

In your discussions you will get a number of comments and opinions that are off base. These can be handled in several ways. You can make a mental note of off-base contributions to the discussion, and then when you are wrapping up the discussion or introducing biblical insight into the discussion, you can correct those off-base opinions or present an alternative viewpoint. This needs to be done in a way that does not put down any of your group members. Another way to handle those off-base opinions is to probe them with questions that push the group to think. Again, this must be done in a responsible way so that the group feels safe in continuing to share their personal opinions. Any time members of the group do not feel safe in sharing their views they will often say only things that they think you, the leader, want to hear. You may be satisfied by their spiritual responses, but will the discussion actually produce changed lives?

We shortchange children when we believe they can't handle discussion or probing questions. Children are more capable than adults often think they are and need opportunities for healthy discussions that consider their problems.

Zinger Discussion Ground Rules

One of the best ways we have found to build this type of acceptance with and among young people is by creating ground rules that guide your discussion. You can begin your discussion by brainstorming a few rules with your group. It helps to write the rules down and post them for everyone to see, as you may need to refer back to them during the discussion.

Keep the number of ground rules to a minimum. Here are some suggested ones that you may want to incorporate into your rules:

1. "What is said in this room stays in this room." Confidentiality is primary if young people are ever to trust you. If you rush off to tell their parents that they once cheated on a spelling test, you will never see them open up again in your group. Confidentiality should only be broken when children reveal they are going to do harm to themselves or another person or when someone is harming them.

2. "Only one person talking at a time." If each person's opinion is worth being heard, the group can demonstrate this by actively listening to everyone who talks. Side talk (talking with the person beside you when it is someone else's turn to speak) is one form of a put-down.

3. "There is no such thing as a dumb question." All questions are legitimate. When young people know they can ask their questions without fear, you have earned their trust and respect!

4. "No one can be forced to talk." Give everyone the right to pass on any question asked of them. This keeps the discussion safe.

5. "All opinions are worth hearing." This means no put-downs, laughing, or rude comments. Disagreement about a group member's opinion can be expressed without attacking the person. Keep the discussion focused on the opinion, not on the person expressing it.

Motivators for Discussion

By using tested leadership discussion skills you can motivate your group to learn by working through a Zinger together. The following are discussion skills that will help you facilitate a healthy discussion.

1. Interacting. It will be difficult for your group to positively interact with each other if they are seated in rows. It will be equally difficult for them to interact if they are scattered throughout the room: some in chairs, a few on a couch, others standing, and the rest on the floor. For optimal interaction ask your group to sit in a circle where each member can see the faces of all the others.

The size of the group also affects interaction. As a rule of thumb, the smaller the group, the more likely people will interact. If you find that only a few children speak, break into smaller groups for a discussion, then come together as a large group for a closure statement.

Encourage all group members to participate in the discussion. When one person (and that includes you) monopolizes the group time, the discussion gets bogged down quickly. If you are having difficulty involving everyone, have a Nerf ball or other soft foam ball on hand. Whenever the ball is thrown to someone, that person gives an opinion or answers a question. It is a useful way to involve more group members in the discussion in a nonthreatening way.

2. Supporting. All good discussions occur in an atmosphere of openness. Allow your group members the freedom to express their points of view without punishment. Young people need to feel safe in sharing their opinions and answers. If kids are penalized through sarcasm, put-downs, or other forms of belittlement, your discussion will die. Examples of support include: "That's an interesting way of looking at the situation." "That's a good idea. Are there any other ideas?" "That's one way of looking at it." Examples of non-support include: "That's the wrong answer!" "Can anyone think of a better answer?" "That's stupid." "Use your brain."

3. Guiding. Many discussions fail because they are nothing more than bull sessions. For a good discussion to occur— one that produces healthy spiritual growth—it is imperative that you identify and work toward a goal or goals. Before beginning your discussion, complete the following three sentences to help structure your Zinger discussion toward a goal or goals:

a. My goal(s) for the session is (are) . . .

b. For this goal to be reached, I must . . .

c. The things that might keep me from reaching my goal are . . .

The discussion must be focused toward a particular goal or goals. Even when you move away from the main point and focus on a tangential issue you are still working toward a goal. It is scattered dialogue that you want to avoid.

Another danger which parallels the bull session and will program your discussion for failure is the gripe session. Your kids will often focus an inordinate amount of their discussion time on the negative when they are telling their stories. They will spend time gossiping about others, bad-mouthing their families, or rambling on about negative movies they have seen. Some negative evaluations are inevitable and even necessary, but do attempt to keep the entire discussion from becoming a gripe session. Keep a balance between the negative comments and positive solutions.

To keep the discussion moving, summarize the points made in the discussion, suggest moving in another direction, ask questions that redirect the discussion, or point out the time limit to your group.

4. Humor. Keep the discussion user-friendly. You will want to allow for jokes and fun during the discussion. As long as the laughter is not from put-downs, lighten the talk with humor.

5. Pausing. Silence makes many people uncomfortable. But silence is an important ingredient for a successful discussion. Pausing for ten to thirty seconds after a question has been asked gives young people time to formulate their thoughts. Do not be afraid of silence. Use it to give kids time to reflect on what has been said and what has been asked.

6. Educating. Periodically, the group members will need to be given new information to help them grow. You will need to introduce new ideas, Scripture passages, or doctrinal teaching into the discussion. Keep it brief. There is not much room for lecture in the discussion method.

7. Probing. This is a tough skill to put into practice. It is the art of getting the group to dig deeper into an issue. Probing is done through questioning, clarifying, and summarizing. Probe with questions of the how and why type (see next section). When young people appear confused about a direction the discussion has taken, ask for clarity or clarify the meaning yourself. Examples of asking for clarity include: "What is another way of saying that?" "Apply that to your situation." "Could you be specific about what you mean by that?" Another way to probe is by asking for a summary of the discussion. Simply ask a group member or two to summarize the discussion that has occurred so far. This will help your group see the flow and direction of the discussion so that you can take it to a deeper level.

8. Facilitating. A big mistake often made by leaders is taking sides in the discussion. Your role should be that of a facilitator. You want to stimulate discussion, which is best done by remaining neutral. You get your opportunity to present your views during the closure of the discussion.

9. Monitoring. At times you may need to step out of your role as facilitator and intervene in the discussion. The following are three useful guidelines to help you decide when to intervene:

a. Gross errors of truth that appear to be confusing many of the group members and are being accepted as fact are a signal that you may need to interrupt the group and clarify the errors. Do this without lecturing or put-downs. See if you can get the children to clarify the confused thinking without your doing so.

b. Continuous departure from the issue or issues being discussed should signal that the group does not understand the goal of the discussion and needs to be put back on track. You can ask the group to define the purpose of the discussion. Or there may be another more pressing issue that needs to be discussed. In that case redirect the discussion to deal with this new issue.

c. Destructive behavior by members toward others in the group should signal the need to return to the Zinger ground rules.

The Right Questions for Discussion

Questioning is best developed through experience. You will improve your question-asking ability the more you practice. There are, however, several tips we can offer you on the art of asking questions.

1. Try to warm up the group at the beginning of the discussion by getting everyone to say something, even if it is only their names. Ask a yes or no question that everyone can respond to as a group.

2. Ask questions clearly enough for everyone to hear and understand.

3. When an individual responds to a question, have her or him talk to the group. Often children will direct their answers to the leader, but this does not facilitate good discussion. Redirect answers given to you to the whole group.

4. Begin with easy, nonthreatening questions, then move to deeper, more probing questions.

5. Allow time for the group to debrief, debate, and process answers to questions rather than your doing so. After Mary answers a question, ask John what he thinks about Mary's response.

6. Gather several responses to one question before evaluating any of the responses.

7. Take a deeper look at responses to a question by probing for the whats, whys, and hows.

8. Throw out the question to the group, then allow time (even a few seconds) for the members to ponder the question before calling on someone specific to respond.

9. Prepare questions of your own. Do not feel locked into the questions provided in the Leader's Tips. Questions you prepare help you tailor the discussion to the needs of your group.

10. Do not answer all the questions yourself, even when questions are directed toward you. Redirect questions to the group.

11. Allow and encourage each group member to ask questions of the group. Do not get into a rut where the group expects you to ask all the questions.

12. Balance the distribution of questions between volunteers and non-volunteers. Do give group members the right to pass on answering a question.

13. If members are not sharing, you may want to try breaking into smaller groups.

14. Encourage, but do not force, kids to answer questions. If a child cannot answer a question, you have two directions you can go. First, you can prompt the individual with hints and clues or rephrase the question and ask the child to look at the issue in a different way. The second choice you have is to move to another group member or go to another question. If you choose to do this to keep the momentum and group interest, do so without embarrassing the individual.

15. Vary the types of questions you ask. There are several types of questions you can use:

a. Recall-level questions require your group to remember certain facts or information. "Who wrote the book of Romans?" or "What story from the Bible did we study last week?" are examples of recall-level questions. Use these questions to take knowledge your group already has acquired and apply it to the present issue being discussed. If you are discussing parents you might ask the question, "When we talked about the family three weeks ago, what is one thing we learned about parents?"

b. Comprehension-level questions measure understanding. They call on your group to translate, give in their own words, restate, paraphrase, illustrate, explain, or give an example. "Could someone please paraphrase the Scripture that was read?" or "Could you say that in your own words?" are examples of comprehension questions.

c. Application-level questions push for transferring what was learned to new situations. They call on your group to respond, demonstrate, apply, relate, or generalize. "Now that we have learned that . . . what are we going to do?" is an application question.

d. Process-level questions ask your group to analyze and synthesize. They call on your group to compare and contrast, deduce, formulate, or develop. You may ask something like, "Why do so many children have trouble with lying?"

e. Evaluation-level questions call for your group to pass judgment. They require your group to choose, decide, evaluate, judge, consider, select, argue, or appraise. An example would be, "Is lying to your parents right or wrong?"

16. Evaluate the questions you ask at the end of the session. Ask yourself if your questions stimulated thinking, created further questions, helped achieve the goals of the session, and kept the interest of the group. This self-evaluation will help you advance your questioning skills.

HOW TO USE A ZINGER

Zingers are fun to do with kids. Zingers are flexible, easy to use, and require little preparation. Use the following four steps to make your Zinger discussions a success.

Zinger Preparation

Once you have chosen the Zinger you wish to discuss, thoroughly read your selection. Read through the Leader's Tips following the Zinger. Each Leader's Tips contains:

1. Topic(s): This gives you an idea about the issue or issues addressed in the Zinger. Because a Zinger is a slice of life, many topics are addressed. You may choose to focus on an issue addressed in the Zinger but not listed under the topic.

2. Purpose: Briefly describes the intent of the Zinger discussion. You may wish to redesign the purpose to fit your group's needs.

3. Questions: Here you will find tips that can help you process the questions from the Kid Question sheets with your kids. You need not feel limited to just these questions. These questions are given as teasers to help you get started in your discussion of the Zinger. You will think of additional questions as you facilitate the discussion.

4. Bible Story: You will find commentary on how to use the Bible story "Let's pretend" activity. A passage of Scripture that offers a story or biblical teaching helps your group examine what God says about the situation and helps your group apply biblical principles to the situation.

5. Additional Scriptures: Biblical passages are given that you can refer to in supplementing the main passage of Scripture.

Before you use the Zinger, talk yourself through the discussion, adding or subtracting your own questions and Scripture. Make copies of the Zinger story for each of the groups who will be discussing it. You can make copies for each member in attendance if paper airplanes, spit wads, and paper snowball fights are not a problem in your group. We have given you permission to photocopy Zingers for your group. Please do not abuse this privilege by making copies for every children's ministry in your city.

Zinger Presentation

The easiest way to introduce a Zinger is to announce to the group that you (or some other group member) will be reading a problem story. The group's job will be to look at the situation and figure out how it could best be handled. Then briefly talk over the ground rules your group will use to guide the discussion.

Read the Zinger story; then break into groups for the Zinger discussion. The larger your group, the more small groups you will want to divide into. We recommend groups of no more than five to ten. You can conduct a Zinger discussion with larger groups but understand that you will have many young people left out of the discussion. You may want to divide into same-sex groupings depending upon the subject being discussed and the needs of your group.

Zinger Guided Discussion

Once the Zinger has been read, the group can answer the questions on the Kid Question sheet. You can photocopy one for each group or for each member of your group. Each Kid Question sheet has four questions with multiple-choice answers. There are no right or wrong answers, although some of the answers are off-base to keep the discussion moving and to sharpen the

discernment and critical thinking skills of your children. Tell the kids that they can choose more than one of the multiple choice answers.

Try to generate as many responses as possible. Your group can consider answers other than the ones provided on the Kid Question sheet. From this interaction your group members will begin to share their stories that are similar to the Zinger situation. It is important to foster this sharing time experience. You may want to say something like, "Are there any of you who have similar things happen to you or your friends? Could you share your story with the group?" You will want to maintain boundaries in the kinds of stories told. You do not want kids to glorify their sins or exaggerate the truth. You do want kids to feel free to talk about their own experiences, both good and bad.

In addition to the use of questions you will find brainstorming, five by fives, and role-plays valuable tools in guiding your group through a Zinger discussion.

Brainstorming is a simple technique that will help your group generate numerous opinions or solutions to a situation or problem. The leader begins the brainstorming session by stating the situation or problem and asking the group to consider as many ideas as possible. Here are several principles to guide your brainstorm sessions.

1. Quantity is more important than quality. List as many ideas as possible without passing judgment on any of them.

2. There should be no put-downs or criticism of anyone's ideas.

3. Encourage group members to piggyback or build upon each other's ideas to create new ideas.

4. Once all ideas have been collected you can go back and group the ideas together into themes, evaluate the ideas, and come to some sort of consensus opinion or solution.

The five by five is another simple yet effective technique that can help your young people generate ideas, choose positions on issues, or solve problems. Simply divide your group into groups of five people each. Tell each group they have five minutes to discuss the Zinger and come up with a solution. One young person in each group should be selected to summarize and report his or her group's thinking to the larger group. Allow less time for groups with younger members.

Role-playing is a technique you will find useful when you want to safely try out a skill, like saying no to peer pressure in a true-to-life situation. Role-plays involve real situations that your group members act out to practice how they would handle the situation. Role-playing should only be used in groups who are well acquainted and trust each other. Here are four guiding principles to help you with Zinger role-plays.

1. Use the Zinger situation or similar stories told to the group by the children as your role-play situation.

2. Pick volunteers from your group to spontaneously act out the situations.

3. Ask the volunteer(s) who is practicing a new skill to try it out during the role-play.

4. Debrief the role-play with a large group discussion about what happened, including suggestions to the volunteer practicing the skill.

Zinger Bible Story Wrap-up

The Bible story page can be photocopied and read by a group member or yourself. The purpose of the Bible story is to wrap up the discussion with a practical examination of the Bible. We have tried to create twists to the Bible stories that relate the Scripture and biblical characters to the lives of your kids today.

Once you have completed the question or questions related to the "Let's pretend" section of the Bible story, you have the opportunity to challenge the group with your concluding remarks. As you consider your conclusion, ask yourself what one or two thoughts you will want your group members to leave the session remembering. End on an affirming high note full of love and hope. Be sure to let your kids know of your availability to talk with them individually after the session concerning issues that may be bothering them.

CHOOSING THE RIGHT ZINGER FOR YOUR GROUP

The Zingers in this book were selected from the stories seven- to ten-year-old young people told us. We listened to the growing-up dilemmas of kids and parents in both urban and suburban settings. We included minority, upper class to lower class, Christian and non-Christian kids in our sampling of stories. Just because a Zinger is found in this book does not mean it is appropriate for your group. All of the issues confronted in Zingers are true-to-life situations that face seven- to ten-year-olds but maybe not your seven- to ten-year-olds. The following eight principles will help you choose the right Zinger to meet the needs of your group.

1. Know the kids in your group well. Children's workers need to be aware of the issues confronting their kids. Since the seven- to ten-year-old is confronted by issues new for adults, it is only natural that workers feel uncomfortable with or are unaware of them. When you are choosing a Zinger, it is imperative that you know the issues confronting the kids with whom you work. In spite of the homogenizing influence of television, there are still community and group differences among kids.

2. Use wise judgment when choosing a Zinger. Some of the Zinger topics may be misunderstood or viewed as controversial. When you risk venturing into "uncharted discussion waters," you risk the criticism of others. Adults in your church, school, club, or wherever you are using Zingers may feel uncomfortable with your talking with children about some of the Zinger issues found here.

There are times when you will find it better to not use a Zinger until you can educate potential critics about the necessity of discussing certain topics. Enlist the help of allies who can support you in educating adults about the new issues created by the growing-up-too-fast syndrome. Then you can proceed with a base of support rather than controversy.

3. Use Zingers as "Talk Treats." Like any other teaching technique, Zingers can be overused. We suggest that you use Zingers as a treat for your group. Pull them out when they supplement your Sunday school curriculum topic. Or use them as a special talk treat at one of your club meetings. Or if you are a classroom teacher, use them sporadically throughout the year to spark a good values discussion.

We have offered you a wide variety of Zingers from which to choose. You do not need to use all of them. Keep them special. Flexible and adaptable, Zingers can be used in any children's group setting, from scout meetings to the Sunday school to the school classroom.

4. Do not use Zingers to contribute to the "growing-up-too-fast" syndrome. In our zeal to help children deal with the realities of their world, we can sometimes contribute to the very things we are against. You must be careful not to create conflict and tension with issues for the sake of shocking kids. We need to present and deal with issues on the children's developmental level. We need not become preoccupied with the ugliness of divorce, death and suffering, adult themes of violence, and other such issues. However, we do need to focus on those issues that confront our kids in their daily lives. In our striving to protect them from the realities of adult life, we can leave them without the tools to deal with the realities of their lives. Seven- to ten-year-olds also need solid answers to help them cope with the realities of their world. Teenagers can deal with ambiguity, but children need concrete answers. Leaving them hanging or confused only serves to push them toward premature adulthood with its cynicism, mistrust, and loss of innocence.

5. Involve parents. It is absolutely necessary to include parents in your choice of Zingers. Children's workers are partners with parents in teaching values and helping kids work through the dilemmas they face. Let's look at a practical example. Parents in one church may not see the need to talk with first graders about movie choices, but these parents may want their third-graders to discuss this issue. The best method for choosing any of the Zingers in this book is to ask for the parents' input on issues they consider important for discussion.

One great way of keeping parents informed about your Zinger discussions is to provide them with copies of the Zingers you wish to use. You may also want to do the same for other adults to whom you are accountable, such as Christian education committees, club leaders, or principals.

Finally, you can send a copy of the Zinger home with each of your kids with instructions to discuss them with their parents. This can be especially effective if parents know ahead of time and are prepared for a discussion time with their sons or daughters.

6. Lift the needs of your group to God in prayer. You may be surprised how God can reveal the needs of your group to you if you will only ask!

7. You are the final authority in choosing a Zinger. Some of the Zingers found in this book can be used with your third and even fourth graders, but not your first and second graders. Others can be used with first, second, and third graders together as a group. Keep in mind that you ultimately are the one who must decide what issues your group needs to discuss and what issues your group is not yet ready to handle. If you enter into a partnership with your children and parents you will be able to use that authority wisely.

THE VCR IS SWEARING

"Come on, Todd, I started the movie," called Sam as he punched the play button on the VCR.

Todd came in from the kitchen with the sodas. *This is great,* he thought. *Sodas, popcorn, and a great movie.*

The movie was a good one, but the language was pretty bad in some parts. Sam did not seem to mind, but Todd was uncomfortable. His parents had told him it was wrong to use those words.

Sam's parents knew he watched movies like this and they didn't seem to mind. In fact, they even watched a few of them together as a family. Sam had great parents. They wouldn't do anything that was wrong for him, would they?

Todd's parents didn't use these words, but his brother did. So what was the big deal? Why shouldn't he use words like that? It didn't seem to bother other kids his age. Todd was very confused.

THE VCR IS SWEARING

Directions: Read each of the following questions. After each question, read and circle the answers. You can circle more than one of the answers if you wish.

1. **What do you think about kids watching movies with bad language?**
   a. It is no big deal.
   b. My mother would be mad if she knew I did it.
   c. As long as I don't get caught it is okay.
   d. I don't think it is right.

2. **Is it really wrong to use bad language?**
   a. No, it is just words.
   b. It is wrong. God does not like it.
   c. I don't know. My family says it is wrong, but my friends say it is not.

3. **Why do some people use bad words?**
   a. I don't know.
   b. Everyone does it.
   c. It's cool.
   d. To show off.

4. **What could you do when you are watching a movie and there is bad language?**
   a. Keep watching the movie and pretend not to hear the words.
   b. Turn the movie off.
   c. Talk with your mom or dad about the movie.
   d. Just watch the movie.

DANNY'S DILEMMA
DANIEL 1:5-8

King Nebuchadnezzar, Neb for short, required the young people working for him to eat food that Neb had first offered to false gods. Daniel, Danny for short, knew God loved him very much. If Danny ate Neb's food he would be worshiping a god who was not real. And Danny knew that the God of the Bible was the real God. Most of the other young people ate Neb's food. Danny had a tough decision to make! It was confusing to figure out what was the best thing to do. He decided not to eat King Neb's food. Instead, he chose a food that had not been given to false gods. Danny knew that God was happy about this choice. And he felt good about what he decided even though it was hard to do. Danny went on to be a very famous person in the Bible.

Let's pretend that instead of eating the King wanted to watch a movie. Neb wanted the young people who worked for him to watch a movie with him. So he had the "royal video renter" go and grab some movies. Danny and the King sat down to watch. The movie started. The King liked it. Danny liked it. Then there was some bad language. Danny had a tough decision to make. What would he do? Danny knew God would not like it if he talked like that. But so many people used bad language . . .
Danny was confused! What do you think Daniel of the Old Testament should do?

19

THE VCR IS SWEARING

TOPIC: INAPPROPRIATE LANGUAGE IN MOVIES

Group: _____

Date Used: _____

Purpose:

This Zinger can help you talk with children about movies that contain inappropriate language as well as other questionable content. Usually, morally questionable movies can best be covered by focusing on the language used, since most contain inappropriate language. In this way there is not a need to talk at length about the violence and sexual content.

You can also use this Zinger to talk about profanity versus appropriate language.

Questions:

1. What do you think about kids watching movies with bad language?

Since so many kids are watching these kinds of movies, move carefully. You can confuse kids more since many of their parents let them watch these kinds of movies. You do not want to be a source of further confusion. Other kids will have parents who do not allow this, and they think all parents are like theirs.

2. Is it really wrong to use bad language?

Ask the kids if they think words can hurt. Ask for examples of how kids have been hurt by words. Explain that bad words are words that can hurt people. Words can also hurt God, like taking his name in vain (Exodus 20:7). Explain that many people do not realize what they are saying when they use bad language. If they did, they may not talk like that.

3. Why do some people use bad words?

People use bad words to get attention, to pretend they are grown up, to be mean, to shock others, to make others angry, to release tension when they are frustrated or stressed. Ask the kids what other things people could say instead of saying bad words.

4. What could you do when you are watching a movie and there is bad language?

Use the following questions to help the group find things they can do. Why do you think Todd was confused about watching a movie where there was bad language? Do you think Todd did the right thing? What else could Todd have done? How could he have obeyed his parents?

Bible Story:

Read through "Danny's Dilemma." Explain what a dilemma is to the group. Tell the group that sometimes we find ourselves in dilemmas like Daniel or Todd did. Gather the group in a circle and brainstorm all of the ways Daniel could have used good judgment. Some possible responses are: (1) turn off the movie and talk with the King about why they should not watch it; (2) turn off the movie and suggest to the King that they do something else; (3) talk with his mother or father about the movie when he went home; (4) watch a different movie.

Additional Scriptures: Proverbs 15:28; Ephesians 5:4; Philippians 4:8

LESLIE'S STUFF

Cara really liked her friend Leslie. They had only known each other a few weeks, and today was the second time Leslie had asked Cara to come over to play at her house.

Cara loved playing at Leslie's. Leslie had everything a kid could want. Cara had seen all of Leslie's toys on the commercials during Saturday morning cartoons.

It was fun to play with Leslie's things even if it was just for a little while. Cara's mom did not believe in buying things that she felt Cara didn't need. If Cara wanted something special she had to earn the money to buy it by doing extra chores around the house.

Cara walked up to Leslie's front door and rang the bell.

"Cara, hi, come on in!" said Leslie as she opened the door. "I've been waiting for you. Come see what I just got."

Leslie led Cara back to her bedroom. "There it is," said Leslie. "What do you think?"

Next to Leslie's bed was the most beautiful doll house Cara had ever seen. It was a two-story with wallpaper on the walls and carpet on the floors. Each room had furniture and little lights that really worked. There was even a little doll family.

"But Leslie," said Cara, "you already have a doll house. We played with it last week."

"Oh, that old thing!" said Leslie as she rearranged the tiny furniture in one of the rooms. "My dad put it out in the garage."

LESLIE'S STUFF

Directions: Read each of the following questions. After each question, read and circle the answers. You can circle more than one of the answers if you wish.

1. **Why do you think Cara liked her new friend Leslie?**
    a. Leslie was popular at school.
    b. Leslie had everything a kid could want.
    c. Leslie shared her stuff with Cara.
    d. Leslie wanted to be more like Cara.

2. **Why do you think Cara's mom didn't believe in buying many things for her?**
    a. She wanted Cara to earn money to buy her own things.
    b. She didn't want to spoil Cara.
    c. She was being mean to Cara.
    d. She didn't care about Cara.

3. **Why do you think Leslie wanted so much stuff from her dad?**
    a. She was selfish.
    b. She thought that's how her dad showed he cared.
    c. She wanted lots of things so she could get more friends.
    d. Everybody else got lots of material things and she wanted to be like everyone else.

4. **How much stuff do you believe God wants us to own?**
    a. As much as we want.
    b. Hardly anything at all.
    c. Anything that will make us happy.
    d. What we need.

A RICH MAN TALKS TO JESUS
LUKE 18:18-30

Once upon a time there was a really rich man who was sad. He was a good man, but he still didn't feel close to God. He would go to the temple and ask God to make him feel better. But nothing ever happened. There were many times when he was happy. After all, he could buy anything he wanted. And that made him feel good.

His friends were confused. They couldn't understand why he was sometimes sad. They knew if they had lots of money and could buy anything they wanted, they would be happy forever.

The rich man heard that Jesus was in town so he went to talk with him about his unhappiness. He knew Jesus could make him very happy. Jesus told the rich man that he loved all his things and money more than he loved God. Jesus wanted the rich man to use his money to help other people.

The rich man was still really sad. He loved all of his stuff so much. Jesus was right. The rich man loved his money more than he loved God.

Let's pretend that the rich man had a daughter in second grade.

The rich man's daughter talked with you on the playground about all her nice toys, videos, and other stuff that her dad had bought for her. She wanted to know how much stuff she could keep and how much stuff she should give to kids who don't have very many toys and games. If she asked you what Jesus would want her to do, what would you tell her?

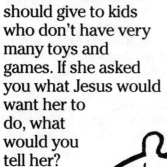

LESLIE'S STUFF
TOPIC: MATERIALISM

Group:_____

Date Used: _____

Purpose:
This Zinger discussion can help you and your kids take a fresh look at our culture's greed and materialism and how Christians can respond to it. Adults often inadvertently teach kids the wrong values about material things. We don't ask ourselves often enough, "What values about material things and money are we communicating to young people through what we do and what we teach?" We need to wrestle with this often ignored issue; this Zinger helps us do just that.

Questions:
1. Why do you think Cara liked Leslie?
After the kids share their responses, explore with them how much Leslie's things contributed to Cara's liking her. Ask the group why they think owning lots of stuff is important to kids.

You can ask your group the following question: If you could have every material thing you wanted, what would you want to have? Then discuss why having so many things is important to kids and adults.

2. Why do you think Cara's mom didn't believe in buying many things for her?
After examining the group's responses, explore with them why buying more and more things can make kids selfish, irresponsible, and ungrateful.

Ask your group what they think of Cara having to earn money by doing extra chores to buy something special that she wanted.

3. Why do you think Leslie wanted so much stuff from her dad?
Each of your kids will be able to relate to this question because they will all have a reason for wanting to get more stuff. Listen to the various stories kids tell. Then explore with the group why they need all the stuff they want from their parents. Don't give the impression that parents can't buy things for kids, but do communicate to your kids that an abundance of material things isn't important for a relationship, whether a parent-child relationship or a friendship.

4. How much stuff do you believe God wants us to own?
What is really important? We often tell kids that money won't buy happiness and then go out and try to prove this axiom wrong by acquiring all of the stuff we can. Explain how our stuff can get in the way of our friendship with God. When we are always worrying about how to get more things, we don't have much time to give to God.

Bible Story:
Kids need to know that money and things can fool them into thinking they are happy. The Bible teaches that materialism is foolish. In this story the rich man was not happy, yet he was unwilling to give up the wealth that was making him unhappy. This, in turn, made him even more unhappy.

Christ was not teaching that it is wrong to have lots of money and material things. Rather, he taught that it is how a person uses what he or she has that makes the difference. Being poor does not make a person more spiritual than the rich, just as being rich is no guarantee of happiness. Your kids need to know that God wants us to use wisely what we have.

Additional Scriptures: Proverbs 10:16; Matthew 6:24; 1 John 2:17

ZINGER 3
PLAYGROUND CONFUSION

Carly stood with her friends in their usual spot on the playground. They talked and watched the other kids until the bell rang.

Carly, Lynne, and Tonya had been friends since school started this year. They were in the same third grade class.

"He's doing it again," said Carly.

"What are you talking about?" asked Lynne.

"That big kid is stealing that first grader's lunch. I saw him do it last week, too!" Carly said. "Someone should do something about it."

"You mean be a tattletale?" asked Tonya.

"I mean tell the playground monitor," said Carly.

"That's what I said, Carly, be a tattletale," Tonya said. "That's what everyone will call you."

"Us too," said Lynne, "since we hang around with you."

"So," Carly said, "what's wrong with that? That poor kid is too little to do anything about it himself."

Tonya answered, "Forget it, Carly. If it bothered the little kid that much he'd tell the monitor himself."

"Yeah," said Lynne, "think about us too."

Carly was confused. *I don't want to be a tattletale,* she thought. *Maybe it doesn't bother that little kid or he would tell someone. Unless he's too scared.*

Carly looked at her friends as she tried to decide what to do.

PLAYGROUND CONFUSION

Directions: Read each of the following questions. After each question, read the answers and circle one. You may circle more than one answer if you wish.

1. What do kids usually do when they are confused about a situation?
 a. Talk with a parent or adult they can trust.
 b. Don't talk with anyone.
 c. Talk with a friend.
 d. Try to forget about it.

2. What do you think would happen if Carly told a teacher about the bully and the first grader?
 a. She would be called a tattletale.
 b. The teacher might be able to help the first grader and the bully.
 c. Other kids would get protection from the bully.
 d. Nothing.

3. What else could Carly do about her confusion?
 a. Talk with her mom or dad.
 b. Not do anything.
 c. Pray to God.
 d. Talk with her Sunday school teacher.

4. Why is it sometimes hard to talk with an adult about kid problems?
 a. Adults give too many lectures.
 b. Kids might get into trouble.
 c. Adults won't always listen.
 d. Adults don't have time to talk.

YOUNG SOLOMON
PROVERBS 4:1-4

You may have heard of King Solomon. God made him the wisest man on earth. But have you heard any stories about King Solomon's childhood? He was a kid at one time. All adults were.

Solomon's father was King David, and Solomon grew up in a palace. But growing up in a palace didn't protect him from the problems that kids face. His father, David, gave him some good advice about facing problems: pay attention to what grown-ups, especially parents, have to say.

Of course, adults are not perfect. They make mistakes. They have problems. They even get confused. Solomon's dad talks in the Bible about his adult mistakes and problems and confusion. But adults can give kids guidance. David told Solomon to listen to grown-ups because adults can give advice from their experiences that can help kids.

Adults know things that kids don't. And kids know things that adults don't. Together, kids and adults can help each other with the confusion and problems of being a kid. But kids must talk with adults to get this help. Perhaps Carly, Lynne, Tonya, the first grader, and the bully could benefit from talking with a grown-up.

Let's pretend that young Solomon was confused because some kids at his school made fun of a boy named Sam who was not good at sports.

Sam had trouble in P.E. class. He always was picked last for a team. The teacher made the other kids let Sam play on the team. Solomon knew Sam felt sad and hurt by the names kids called him. Solomon did not know how to be friends with Sam. If he played with Sam, the other kids might make fun of Solomon.

Why do you think Solomon was so confused about Sam? How might Solomon's father help him with his confusion?

LEADER'S TIPS
PLAYGROUND CONFUSION
TOPIC: WHO TO TALK TO WHEN YOU'RE CONFUSED

Group:_____

Date Used: _____

Purpose:
Being a kid in an adult's world can be bewildering. Today's kids are exposed to adult-strength confusion from television, difficult family living situations, and even from other kids at school. The problem in this Zinger is mild compared to many that kids face today. Yet this Zinger can help you and your group talk together about how kids can face confusion today.

Questions:
1. What do kids usually do when they are confused about a situation?
Give your group members the chance to talk about all the ways kids handle confusing situations. Your kids will want to tell stories about how they and their friends have handled tough, confusing times.

2. What do you think would happen if Carly talked with a teacher about her confusion over what to do about the bully and the first grader?
Walk your group through each of the possibilities, including ones that are not on the worksheet. Discuss the difference between a tattletale and a helper. Most tattling is done to get attention. But there are times when kids need to talk with adults about peers who are hurting themselves or others. Examine the difference between getting another kid in trouble and getting someone help.

3. What else could Carly do about her confusion?
Use this opportunity to encourage kids to talk with adults about important topics. Many children keep their confusion to themselves. Others talk with their friends. Both responses exclude adults. Young people today are more and more separated from adults. We don't want kids to think that they can't talk with their friends about problems. Rather, we want children to see that they can also talk with adults—parents, teachers, aunts and uncles, and Sunday school teachers. Don't forget to encourage young people to talk with God, asking for his guidance.

4. Why is it sometimes hard to talk with an adult about kid problems?
Fortunately, most kids can and do talk with adults. You can use this opportunity to reinforce the need to develop relationships with and learn from parents and other trustworthy adults. Give your group a chance to air their gripes about the lack of adult involvement in their lives.

5. Why is it good to talk with adults even though it is difficult?
Brainstorm ways kids can involve adults more in their lives after you have talked about benefits of talking with adults. Debunk the myth that kids are not as smart as adults. Adults can and need to learn from kids. And kids need to take advantage of adult experience.

Bible Story:
You can wrap up your discussion by examining the Bible story reinforcing parental and adult wisdom. Ask the group to picture what it might have been like to be a kid during Bible times, perhaps the son or daughter of a famous Bible character. Help them see that being a kid in Bible times was not so different from being a kid today. King David had to encourage his son to listen to adults just like you are encouraging the group to do.

You can tell a story about a time in your childhood when you faced a situation where you didn't know what to do. Ask the kids to help you complete the story, considering what God would have wanted.

Additional Scriptures: Proverbs 10:23; 15:14; 28:26

PEER PRESSURE

"Come on, Brad," said Matthew.

Here we go again, thought Brad. The last time Matthew came over he tried to talk Brad into letting him borrow the new toy truck Brad's dad just gave him. Now he was doing it again.

"You know, Brad," said Matthew, "you say I'm your best friend. If my best friend wanted to borrow one of my trucks, I would let him. You are just being selfish."

"But Matthew, my dad just bought me this truck."

Brad's dad was a truck driver. Whenever he saw something interesting on one of his trips he would bring it home to Brad.

"This truck is really special. It looks almost like the one my dad drives!" said Brad. "He'd be really sad if I let you take it. He made me promise to keep it in a safe place."

"I'm not going to take it forever," said Matthew. "I'll just play with it for a few days, and then you can have it back. Besides, your dad won't know unless you tell him."

Brad thought about it for a few minutes. "What if you break it?" he asked. "My dad would really be hurt! The last time you borrowed one of my toys you broke it."

"Brad, you worry too much," Matthew said. "He won't be that upset. It's just a toy. Next time you come over to my house you can borrow one of mine."

I guess he's right, thought Brad. *It is just a toy.*

"Okay, Matthew," he said, "but you better take good care of it."

PEER PRESSURE

Directions: Read each of the following questions. After each question, read the answers and circle one. You may circle more than one answer if you wish.

1. Why was the truck important to Brad?
   a. It was new.
   b. It was like his father's truck.
   c. His father bought it for him.
   d. It belonged to him.

2. Why would Matthew keep asking for the truck?
   a. He wanted Brad to prove he was a friend.
   b. Matthew was jealous.
   c. Matthew didn't like Brad's dad.
   d. Matthew doesn't believe in obeying adults.

3. Why do you think Brad gave in?
   a. He was afraid of Matthew.
   b. He didn't want to lose Matthew as a friend.
   c. He didn't feel he had a choice because his dad wasn't there.
   d. He thought that was what friends were supposed to do.

4. What other choices did Brad have?
   a. Tell Matthew no.
   b. Explain that if Matthew really was a friend he would quit asking.
   c. Tell Matthew that he had to ask his father first.
   d. Offer Matthew another toy.
   e. Tell Matthew to go home.

ELIJAH AT YOUR SCHOOL
1 KINGS 18:18-39

Jezebel and the false prophets worshiped a false god named Baal. And they pressured other people to do the same. The king of Israel, Ahab, liked to worship Baal too. King Ahab pressured people to worship Baal even though Baal was just pretend. People living in Bible times had trouble with peer pressure just like people today.

Elijah showed the people that they had been fooled into thinking that Baal was real. Elijah was a true prophet of God. He called on God for a miracle so that the people who were tricked into believing in Baal could see that they were being fooled. And wow, what a miracle! Remember the story?

Let's pretend that Elijah is your age and attends your school for a day. What kinds of things might Elijah be pressured to do by kids at your school? How do you think Elijah might handle these pressures?

31

LEADER'S TIPS
PEER PRESSURE
TOPIC: THE PRESSURE TO CONFORM

Group:_____

Date Used: _____

Purpose:
This Zinger can be used to talk about peer pressure as it relates to a child's desire to fit in and belong with other children.

Questions:
1. Why was the truck important to Brad?
After discussing the different answers, ask the kids if something like this has ever happened to them. Let the kids share their experiences with the group.

2. Why would Matthew keep asking for the truck?
Talk with your group about reasons why kids pressure other kids. Look back at some of the stories your kids shared in response to the first question. It is important to talk about peer pressure in relationship to the "need to be needed" that all of us feel. Adults and kids want to be needed, belong, have friends, and fit in.

3. Why do you think Brad gave in?
Relate this question back to the stories kids told. Ask your group if there are good reasons to give in. Write the phrase "peer pressure" on a chalkboard or newsprint for everyone to see. Ask the group to define it. Explain that peer pressure is a phrase that adults use to describe what happens when people go along with what many other people are doing. There is positive peer pressure to do things that are good and negative peer pressure to do things that are bad.

4. What other choices did Brad have?
Create a master list of all the choices. Then ask your group to choose the best ones. You may want to do a practice role-play in which you and your kids practice saying no in creative ways.

Bible Story:
Review the story of Elijah on Mount Carmel. Point out that not everyone followed the crowd that worshiped Baal. The Bible says that there were 100 prophets (1 Kings 18:3-4) and 7,000 people (1 Kings 19:18) who were still faithful to the true God. That's what we call positive peer pressure.

But Elijah felt he was the only one serving God. It seemed to him that no one else was doing what was right (1 Kings 19:10). Ask the children if they have ever felt like Elijah. Sometimes we may feel like we have to do something wrong because everyone else is doing it. We can then remember this story and realize there are other people doing the right thing!

Ask the kids to answer the question, "What kinds of things might Elijah be pressured to do by kids at your school?" They can give good and bad things that kids feel pressured into doing. Then talk about ways to resist negative peer pressure.

Additional Scriptures: Psalm 1:1-2; Romans 12:2

THE MOVIE TIME QUESTION

Lorrie was excited. Today her class would find out if they had enough points for a movie time. Each day the class got points for good behavior. Someone could earn extra credit points for the class by helping the teacher or another student. Once the class earned 75 points they could have a movie time with popcorn and other treats they brought from home.

"Okay everybody, settle down," said Ms. Hawks, their teacher. After everyone was quiet, she said, "I'm happy to announce that our class has enough points for a movie time. It will be this Friday."

Cheers of "yeah," "all right," and "cool" came from the kids in the class.

"Today, with Ms. Graham's help, our movie committee will decide on some movies for us to choose from."

Ms. Graham was the mother of one of the kids in the class. She helped out in class once a week. Lorrie, Raoul, and Angela were on the movie committee. They met in the back of the room. Raoul and Lorrie sat together.

"Our job," Ms. Graham said, "is to pick out two movies for the whole class to vote on. I brought a list of G-rated movies for us to choose from."

"G-rated!" the three of them moaned together. "How boring!"

"Hey, Raoul," Lorrie whispered, "what's this G-rated kid stuff? I thought we were going to pick a good movie!"

THE MOVIE TIME QUESTION

Directions: Read each of the following questions. After each question, read the answers and circle one. You may circle more than one answer if you wish.

1. **Why do you think Lorrie, Raoul, and Angela don't like G-rated movies ?**
   a. They think they are too childish.
   b. They think they are boring.
   c. They have seen them already.
   d. They want to watch more exciting stuff.

2. **What kinds of movies are your friends allowed to watch?**
   a. They can watch whatever their parents say they can watch.
   b. They can watch anything they want.
   c. They can watch whatever they want as long as they don't get caught by their parents.
   d. They can watch movies that are good for them.

3. **Why are adults concerned with the kinds of movies kids watch?**
   a. Adults want to be mean to kids.
   b. Adults want to protect kids from bad stuff.
   c. Adults don't want kids to have too much fun.
   d. Adults want to teach kids about grown-up things themselves rather than having kids learn about them from movies.

4. **How can kids best decide the kinds of movies they should watch?**
   a. Kids should watch what their friends watch.
   b. Kids should watch whatever they want.
   c. Kids should watch what they think would be good for them.
   d. Kids should watch what they think Jesus would watch.

HEZEKIAH'S CHOICE
2 KINGS 18:1-8

Hezekiah was a king of Judah. His story is told in the Old Testament. The Bible says Hezekiah was a young man when he became a king. He was faced with a tough decision. Many of the people of Judah had stopped caring about God. They were worshiping false gods. The people of Judah had learned about these false gods from people who lived around their nation.

Hezekiah could have worshiped false gods like most of his people. Instead, he decided to follow the true God. He knew that false gods could not help him or anyone else. He cleaned up the temple and influenced his people to again love God.

It sounds like it was easy for Hezekiah to worship God, but it was not. People laughed at him. Some people thought he was crazy. But Hezekiah knew that his choices were important. If you read the story you will find that Hezekiah's faithfulness to God paid off. He made the right choices. He was a good king.

Let's pretend that Hezekiah could rent movies.

Now Hezekiah had another choice to make. He had to decide what kinds of movies he would watch. He knew that some movies were bad for him just like worshiping false gods. And Hezekiah wanted to do the things that pleased God. What kinds of movies do you think he would choose to watch?

THE MOVIE TIME QUESTION
TOPIC: MOVIE VIEWING CHOICES

Group:_____

Date Used: _____

Purpose:
Not very long ago children used to be protected from bad language, violence, and sexual content in the movies they saw. The release of the movie Bambi stirred quite a controversy among child psychologists because Bambi's mother was killed by hunters. Little attention, let alone controversy, is generated today by young children watching R-rated movies (or worse) on cable or rental videos. The next time you visit your local video rental store, observe which movies kids pick up and hand to their parents for rental. This Zinger can help you discuss the importance of good choices of movies.

Questions:
1. Why do you think Lorrie, Raoul, and Angela don't like G-rated movies?
If need be, explain the ratings to kids. By asking this question, you will get a picture of why kids watch the kinds of shows they do.

2. What kinds of movies are your friends allowed to watch?
Focus on how their friends affect what they watch. Talk about the content of the movies their friends watch.

3. Why are adults concerned with the kinds of movies kids watch?
Be sensitive to the fact that some parents let their kids watch movies with highly questionable content. Do not put the children on the spot by asking how many of them are allowed to watch such and such. When you do this you are forcing kids to make a moral judgment about their parents. As a Christian leader you have a responsibility to help parents in their role.

Focus on adults' desire to protect and train kids in a godly manner. Adults want kids to have Christian character and that can't be gained through watching many of today's movies.

4. How can kids best decide the kinds of movies they should watch?
Spend some time talking about movies' contents in general terms (bad language, violence) and how it affects kids.

Bible Story:
Tell the kids that Hezekiah had life-affecting choices to make. The movie choices kids make affect their lives. Ask the kids if the movies they mentioned in the discussion would be ones that Hezekiah would want to watch. Then discuss how these movies affect them in good and bad ways. Finally, talk about ways kids can influence their friends to watch good movies just like Hezekiah influenced people to love God.

Additional Scriptures: Psalm 51:10; Philippians 4:8

IT'S MY PARTY

"It's my birthday. I can invite who I want to my party," Lila told her mother.

It was Lila's eighth birthday. As a present her parents were throwing a party for her at the local pizza parlor. They told her she could invite anyone she wanted—up to fifteen kids. Lila had decided to invite all the girls in her class. Except one.

"Lila," said her mom, "if you are going to invite all the girls in your class you can't leave one out. Think of how it would make her feel."

"I know, Mom. But I just can't."

"Why don't you want to invite Shelly?" Mom asked.

"She's weird!" Lisa said. "She dresses funny, and her hair is never clean. The kids all make fun of her!"

"Maybe," Mom said, "if you invited her to the party, the other girls would accept her."

"If the other girls find out I invited her, they probably won't come," said Lila. "I don't want to hurt feelings, Mom, but it's my party."

IT'S MY PARTY

Directions: Read each of the following questions. After each question, read the answers and circle one. You may circle more than one answer if you wish.

1. How do you think Shelly will feel if she is not invited?
   a. Hurt.
   b. Angry.
   c. Nothing because she never expected to be invited.
   d. Glad.
   e. Sad.

2. How might Lila's friends react if Lila invites Shelly?
   a. They won't come.
   b. Some will attend the party and some won't.
   c. Some will be glad Shelly was invited.
   d. Lila's friends won't care whether Shelly is invited or not.

3. How might Shelly feel if she were invited?
   a. Surprised.
   b. Happy.
   c. Confused.
   d. Thankful.

4. How can Lila invite Shelly and still keep her friends?
   a. Talk to her other friends first about inviting Shelly.
   b. Blame it on her mom.
   c. Act surprised if Shelly comes.
   d. Talk to her friends after the party about why Shelly needed
       to be invited.

THE CRIPPLE
2 SAMUEL 9:3-13

You may have already heard many stories about David. He lived in Old Testament times. Remember the story about David and Goliath? David was a really famous person in the Bible. One story about David you may have never heard is the story of Mephibosheth. How would you like to have a name like that? Mephibosheth was Jonathan's son. Remember that Jonathan was David's best friend? Mephibosheth's nurse dropped him when he was only five years old. He was unable to walk after that. The Bible says he was crippled in both feet.

We can be sure that Mephibosheth was rejected by many kids when growing up because he was different. This affected him as a child and as an adult. When David visited him, Mephibosheth said a bad thing about himself. We call this a put-down. Mephibosheth did not like himself very much, probably because he had felt rejection most of his life.

David became friends with Mephibosheth instead of rejecting him. He wanted to help Mephibosheth. That doesn't mean Mephibosheth was David's only friend. Or that David spent all of his time with Mephibosheth. But David did like him and didn't make fun of him or reject him.

Let's pretend that David could advise Lila about Shelly. What do you think David would have told Lila about Shelly?

IT'S MY PARTY
TOPIC: REJECTION

Group:_____

Date Used: _____

Purpose:
Anyone who works with seven- to ten-year-olds knows that kids can be cruel to each other, especially to kids who are different. And all kids have both rejected others and been rejected. This Zinger can be used to discuss what it is like to reject and be rejected and how Christians can effectively handle this issue.

Questions:
1. How do you think Shelly will feel if she is not invited?
Children who are rejected, especially on a regular basis, often feel unloved, hurt, sad, angry, unwanted, and unneeded. Ask the young people to talk about times they have been rejected and how it has felt.

2. How might Lila's friends react if Lila invites Shelly?
Let your kids share how their classmates would react. One third grader said he would never invite Shelly because he wasn't popular at school but wanted to be. Inviting Shelly would guarantee that he stayed unpopular. For this third grader, rejecting Shelly was a way to popularity. Some kids reject other kids to build themselves up.

3. How might Shelly feel if she were invited?
Some kids may argue that it would be bad to invite Shelly because she would be rejected at the party and feel worse. Talk with the kids about all the reasons why Shelly might be rejected. Ask the group how often kids get rejected at their school.

4. How can Lila invite Shelly and still keep her friends?
It is important to offer kids strategies that help them realistically deal with this and similar situations. Ask them to creatively consider all the ways they could befriend people like Shelly and still keep their friends. Ask them to consider ways to avoid participating with other kids in rejecting kids that are different. Also discuss ways they can handle being rejected by other kids.

Bible Story:
Ask the kids to give all the reasons why Mephibosheth would have been rejected as a kid. You can make a list of reasons on newsprint or a chalkboard. Ask the kids how Mephibosheth would be treated if he were a student at their school. Then talk about the advice they think King David might give them.

You can also explore times they have felt like Mephibosheth. Talk about times they have felt unloved and put themselves down. This is an opportunity to practice active listening skills. Kids who have experienced rejection need your acceptance and unconditional love.

Additional Scriptures: You can examine how Christ was rejected by summarizing Isaiah 53. Kids should know that their friend Jesus Christ was also rejected.

MISSING HER

"But why did she have to die?" Ryan cried. "Why did she leave me?"

Ryan's mom had just told him his grandmother died in the night. She was a great grandma. She didn't mind getting dirty, and she liked to help Ryan build models. She and Ryan would have long talks while they made chocolate chip cookies. Sometimes Ryan would tell her things he could not even tell his mom or dad. Then they would eat the cookies—as many as he wanted!

"She didn't want to leave you, Ryan. Her heart just got too tired, and yesterday it stopped beating," Mom said as she held Ryan.

"I shouldn't have played so rough with her," Ryan said.

"No, Ryan, she liked to play with you," Mom replied.

"I never got to say good-bye or even tell her I loved her," Ryan cried.

"She knew you loved her, Ryan. Think of all the great times you had together," Mom said.

"I'll miss her," Ryan said, holding Mom tighter.

"Me too," Mom whispered.

MISSING HER

Directions: Read each of the following questions. After each question, read and circle an answer. You can circle more than one answer if you wish.

1. Why did Ryan cry when his grandmother died?
a. He was really scared.
b. He was confused about death.
c. He missed her.
d. He thought her death was his fault.
e. He may not have known anyone who had died before.

2. Should Ryan try to get over his grandmother's death as quickly as he can?
a. Yes, he should forget about it right away so he won't feel sad.
b. He should pretend it never happened.
c. No, he needs to feel lots of different feelings even though it hurts and takes time.
d. No, Ryan needs to talk about his thoughts and feelings with God and someone he trusts. This will help him understand his grandmother's death.

3. What can you do when someone close to you or a pet you love dies?
a. You can remember the good things about that person or pet.
b. You can cry as much as you want.
c. You can talk about all the things you feel with someone who cares about you.
d. You can talk with God about how you feel even if you are mad.
e. You can pretend it didn't happen.

4. How can you help a friend whose grandmother or other loved one has died?
a. You can feel sad with them.
b. You can ignore your friend.
c. You can listen to how he or she feels.
d. You can tell an adult about your friend if you think your friend needs extra help.

JOSEPH'S SAD DAY
GENESIS 50:1-14

Joseph's brothers were mean to him, very mean. They sold him. Have you ever been mean to your brother or sister? Have you ever felt like selling them if you could? The Bible says that Joseph forgave his brothers and they made up. This happened at the end of the story in the book of Genesis.

Something else happened at the end of the story of Joseph. His father died. The Bible says Joseph and his brothers were very sad. They had a funeral for their father and cried and cried.

They were sad and cried because they were grieving. Grieving is when you feel really sad and hurt after you lose someone or something you loved. Grieving is a normal thing people do when someone they love dies. People also grieve or feel sad when a pet they love dies. God knows we love our family, friends, and pets. When one of them dies, he wants us to cry and feel sad. Grieving helps us feel better after a while. But when you are feeling sad and missing the person or pet who died, it is hard to think you will feel better someday.

Joseph didn't stay sad. After a while he began to feel better. One of the things that helped Joseph was his friendship with God. He prayed to God and God helped him feel better. He knew that God loved him very much.

Let's pretend that you could talk to Joseph right now. Joseph learned much about grieving because he lived to be 110 years old. He loved God very much. And God taught him a lot during his lifetime. What do you think Joseph might tell you about grieving?

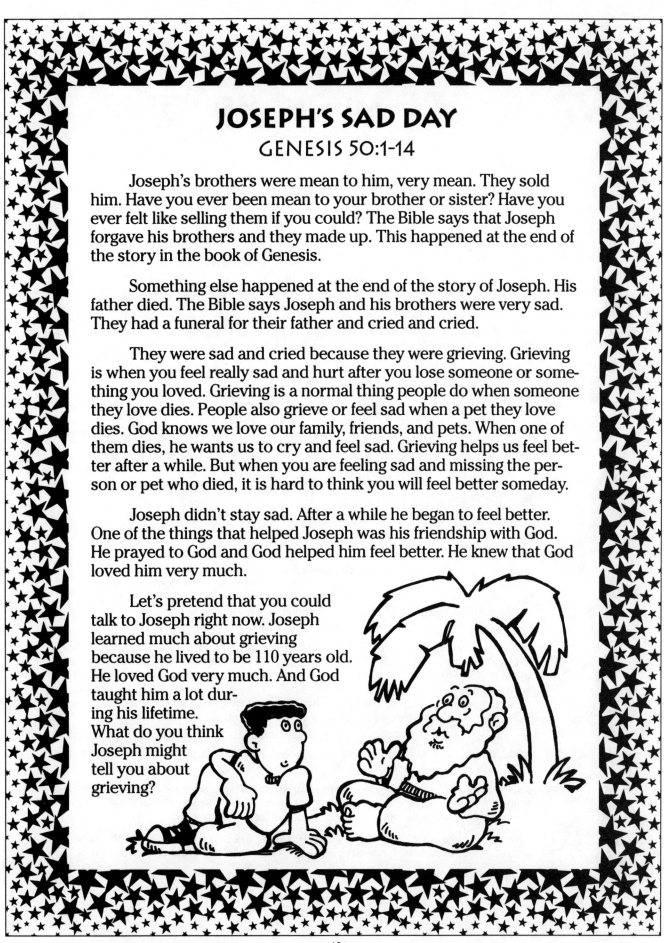

43

LEADER'S TIPS
MISSING HER
TOPIC: DEALING WITH DEATH

Group:_____

Date Used: _____

Purpose:
This is an especially helpful Zinger when there has been a death in your community that touches your group of kids. All kids have questions about death, and you need not avoid them. For most people around the world, death is a common occurrence. But in our high-tech Western world, death is unexpected and frightening. We hide death from people in mortuaries, hospitals, and convalescent centers. Because we are unfamiliar with death, we have difficulty talking about it directly with kids.

Since death, for the Christian, is not the end of life but only the beginning, this Zinger can be used to help explain our faith.

Questions:
1. Why did Ryan cry after his grandmother died?
Discuss all the reasons the kids give. Then give your kids the opportunity to share their experiences. They can talk about the death of a pet or a loved one. Or perhaps one of your kids is experiencing a life-threatening illness that he or she can talk about.

2. Should Ryan try to get over his grandmother's death as quickly as he can?
Grieving a death takes time. Kids need to be encouraged to feel their painful feelings and talk about them. Young people and adults don't just "get over" a death. As the Bible story illustrates, God intended for us to grieve those we have lost. Christians have hope in Christ, but we still grieve.

3. What can you do when someone close to you or a pet you love dies?
In addition to talking about all the positive things that kids can do to cope with a death, take some time to answer kids' questions about death.

4. How can you help a friend whose grandmother or other loved one has died?
Talk with your group about how death can scare us. When we know someone who is sad because of a death, we may also be afraid and not know how to be their friend. Create a list of all the things kids can do to support someone who is sad.

Bible Story:
Children need honest and simple answers and information about death. Use this Bible story to talk about grieving. Explain that we go through different stages of grief. We feel different things at different times after someone or something close to us dies. At first we pretend it never happened. The shock of the tragedy causes people to disbelieve its reality. People who don't understand grief think that kids at this stage are being indifferent or uncaring toward the dead person. But they really are in shock over the death.

After the initial shock wears off, people who are grieving start saying good-bye to the person who has died. They will feel hurt, sad, and lonely. Sometimes they may even think the person is still alive. They may even look for the person or think they see the deceased loved one.

Kids then move from saying good-bye to recognition that their loved one has really died and is gone. They may experience a time of transition marked with anger and confusion before they finally accept the death and move to a new place in their lives.

Grieving is God's way for us to move on and grow in our lives. And kids, like adults, need to grieve when they have lost a loved one or a pet that was an important part of their lives.

Additional Scriptures: Psalm 23; Isaiah 57:2; John 11:25; John 14:1-3; Philippians 3:20-21

LUNCH MONEY TROUBLE

I can't believe I did it again, Amber thought. This was the fourth time in two weeks she had forgotten her lunch money. Not only would she starve again, but she would also have to listen to another lecture on responsibility from her teacher, Ms. Gary. That was worse than not having any lunch.

I know I had it in my pants pocket, she thought. *It must have been those cartwheels I did on the way to school. I guess I should put my money in my backpack like my mom told me. She's going to be mad at me. I could go back home to get it . . . No, then I'd be late and get in just as much trouble.*

As Amber walked up the sidewalk to the school door, she noticed something. There on the grass was a book bag. Beside the bag was a handful of change. Amber looked around the playground. Whoever left the bag was nowhere to be seen.

Amber picked up the money and counted it. Wow! There was enough for her lunch. Amber stared at the money in her hand.

My problems are over, she thought. *The person who left this here should have been more careful. It's not like I'm going to take the backpack. I'll only take enough money for lunch. I can turn the backpack in to the office.*

Amber picked up the backpack. As she walked into the school office, she put the money into her pocket. "Finders keepers, losers weepers," she whispered to herself.

LUNCH MONEY TROUBLE

Directions: Read each of the following questions. After each question, read the answers and circle one. You may circle more than one answer if you wish.

1. Why doesn't Amber have any lunch money?
    a. Amber's mother didn't make sure she put the money in her backpack.
    b. Amber didn't remember her money.
    c. Amber is stupid.
    d. Amber is too young to take care of herself.

2. Is "finders keepers, losers weepers" always true?
    a. Yes, if you lose something, whoever finds it can keep it.
    b. Sometimes. You have the right to keep things you find if you really need them.
    c. No, it's stealing.
    d. If you can't find the owner, you can keep what you find.

3. What could Amber do with the backpack and money she found?
    a. Keep it and not tell anybody.
    b. Leave it where she found it.
    c. Turn the bag and money in to somebody in the school office.
    d. Try to find the owner.

4. Why would it be wrong for Amber to keep the money?
    a. It's stealing, and God says we shouldn't steal.
    b. The owner of the backpack will not be able to buy a lunch.
    c. It doesn't belong to Amber.
    d. It's not wrong.
    e. Amber may have to lie to her mother.

THE EIGHTH COMMANDMENT

EXODUS 20:15

Have you ever wondered why God felt so strongly about people stealing that he made a commandment against it? It is the eighth commandment. You know the Ten Commandments are rules God gave Moses to give to God's people. They help us live together and not sin against God. The Eighth Commandment is very simple but very important. It says "You shall not steal."

What would it be like if there were no Eighth Commandment? What if the Bible had said, "Finders keepers, losers weepers"?

What would it be like at your school if it were okay to steal? What would you do if anyone could take your lunch box, backpack, or books?

Let's pretend that it is okay to steal at your school. If someone wanted to take something that belonged to you, they could without getting in trouble. And you could steal whatever you wanted. What would your school be like? Why is it good that God gave us the Eighth Commandment?

LEADER'S TIPS
LUNCH MONEY TROUBLE
TOPIC: STEALING

Group: _____

Date Used: _____

Purpose:
Most children at this age understand that stealing is wrong, yet it can be a problem. There is a reason why the saying "finders keepers, losers weepers" has been popular among children. It is a justification for keeping something that is not ours to keep. Use this Zinger to explore the problem areas related to stealing your group has experienced.

Questions:
1. Why doesn't Amber have any lunch money?
Kids may want to argue that it is okay for Amber to keep the money. Focus first on the issue of responsibility. Often, we are tempted to take things that aren't ours because we are unwilling to take responsibility for our situations.

Examine all the reasons kids steal things: for excitement; lack of material things; selfishness; feeling empty, lonely, or sad; tough friends; peer pressure.

2. Is "finders keepers, losers weepers" always true?
Ask (and explain, if necessary) what the saying "finders keepers, losers weepers" means. Then have the kids give you situations when it is true and when it is not. Explain that this is never a reason to take something that belongs to someone else. There are times when you find something that can be kept if the owner can't be identified. But in Amber's situation, this is not true.

3. What could Amber have done with the backpack and money she found?
Here is your opportunity to brainstorm solutions with the group. It is good for the kids to see that there is more than one positive solution to this dilemma.

4. Why would it be wrong for Amber to keep the money?
This last question provides you with a good lead-in to the Bible story. Ask the group to list as many answers as they can. Create a master list of all their answers and point out that there are many good reasons not to steal.

Bible Story:
Ask the group how they think God defines stealing. Write down a group definition. Talk about what it would be like if stealing were not against the rules at school. The kids will provide stories that include more than stealing. There will be lying, fighting, cheating, hurt feelings, and broken friendships. In short, things would be a mess. Some kids initially will think it might be fun, but you can ask questions that demonstrate to the group why it was good that God gave us the Eighth Commandment.

Additional Scriptures: Leviticus 6:1-7; Ephesians 4:28

ZINGER 9
JUST A SIP

Troy and Glenn walked through the front door of Glenn's house. Troy was spending the afternoon at Glenn's. They threw their backpacks in the chair as they headed for the kitchen. On the table was a note from Glenn's oldest brother Tim.

"What's it say?" Troy asked.

"It says he went to the store and he'll be right back," Glenn said. "Let's go out back."

Glenn and Troy spent the next hour playing in Glenn's tree house. It was great. They could see almost the whole neighborhood from up there.

"Hey, there's my brother's car. Let's go," Glenn said as he started down the ladder.

"Hey, Tim. This is my friend Troy," Glenn said as they walked into the kitchen.

"Hi, Troy," Tim said, opening the refrigerator. He pulled out a can of beer.

As Glenn and Troy watched, he opened it and took a drink.

"You guys look thirsty," said Tim. "Do you want a drink?"

JUST A SIP

Directions: Read each of the following questions. After each question, read the answers and circle one. You may circle more than one answer if you wish.

1. **Why might Glenn's brother offer Troy and Glenn a drink of his beer?**
   a. He knew they were thirsty.
   b. He wanted to tease them.
   c. He wanted to get them in trouble.
   d. He didn't think it was wrong for kids to drink alcohol.

2. **Why is it not good for kids to drink alcohol?**
   a. Kids are not old enough.
   b. It is not healthy for kids to drink alcohol.
   c. Parents don't like kids to drink.
   d. Drinking alcohol is against the law for kids.

3. **How could Glenn and Troy say no to Tim?**
   a. They could say no and go back outside to play in Glenn's tree house.
   b. They could say they want juice instead.
   c. They could say it is not healthy for kids to drink.
   d. They could say that their parents do not want them to drink alcohol.

4. **Should Glenn and Troy tell their parents about the drink offer?**
   a. No. They should keep it to themselves.
   b. Yes, but only tell Glenn's parents.
   c. Yes, but only tell Troy's parents.
   d. Yes, tell both Glenn and Troy's parents.

A WORD TO THE WISE
PROVERBS 23:29-35

Glenn and Troy had a choice to make. They had to decide whether or not they were going to drink alcohol. Do you think the Bible might be able to help them?

The Bible says that drinking alcohol can be very dangerous. It warns people about the misuse of alcohol in the book of Proverbs. This Old Testament book is a book of good advice. It says alcohol can be like poison from a snake. If you don't believe it, read Proverbs 23:32.

Some kids may think it is okay to drink alcohol, but bad things can happen. When someone drinks alcohol their behavior can change. They may act silly or make a bad decision. Kids who drink can hurt their bodies. Drinking alcohol makes it harder to think straight.

Even though bad things can happen when kids drink alcohol, there are still people who try to talk kids into drinking alcohol such as beer and wine. Older kids may offer younger kids a drink of alcohol. People make commercials on TV that try to get adults and kids to drink alcohol. But just because some people try to get kids to drink doesn't mean kids have to say yes. Smart kids say no to drinking alcohol.

Let's pretend that a TV station wanted you to do a commercial. The commercial you get to make needs to convince kids that they should not drink alcohol. What would you say and do in your commercial?

LEADER'S TIPS
JUST A SIP
TOPIC: ALCOHOL USE

Group: _____

Date Used: _____

Purpose:
This Zinger can be used to reinforce what many kids are already getting at school—a clear "no alcohol" message. You can also take this opportunity to strengthen what most of your kids may be hearing in their families. Begin your discussion by asking your group what they have already learned at home and school. Then ask them to apply what they have learned to help Troy and Glenn with their problem.

Questions:
1. Why might Glenn's brother offer Troy and Glenn a drink of his beer?
Ask the group if there are any situations similar to this where kids are pressured to drink alcohol. Explore how they think older kids might feel pressured. Explain that there may be times when they will feel pressure to take a drink of alcohol. The reason you are having this discussion is to talk about ways kids can say no when they face tough situations like Troy and Glenn did.

2. Why is it not good for kids to drink alcohol?
Kids are more health conscious today than ever before. Explore how unhealthy alcohol can be to them now. Stay with the present since kids have some difficulty extrapolating consequences into the future. Create a list of additional reasons beyond those found on the worksheet. Challenge the group to see how many reasons they can consider.

3. How could Glenn and Troy say no to Tim?
Talk and even practice through role-plays with the kids about saying no. Kids need to know how to say no, and that requires a skill that must be practiced. Each answer on the worksheet offers a strategy for refusing alcohol. See how many more strategies your group can think of. This can help provide your kids with practiced refusal skills that they are ready to use when confronted with a difficult situation.

4. Should Glenn and Troy tell their parents about the drink offer?
Let the group give their opinions. Then talk about the benefits of being honest with their parents about tough situations. There are some things they don't need to tell their parents, but really important issues need to be discussed. You can make a list of those things that they really need to discuss with their parents.

Bible Story:
Your group will be applying what Scripture teaches as they create their commercials. You can break into smaller groups to create your commercials if you have an adult for each small group. The adults can help each group create a list of all the things the kids want said in the commercial, then the kids can provide ideas about what the commercial would look like. The adults can offer assistance in illustrating the commercial. Each group can then describe their commercial to the other groups.

Additional Scriptures: Proverbs 20:1; Ephesians 5:18

ZINGER 10
I DON'T UNDERSTAND

"Dory, you've looked sad all week. What's wrong?" Lydia asked. Dory and Lydia sat beside each other every school day on the bus.

"It's my parents," sighed Dory as she looked down at her shoes. "They're fighting again. They try to hide it by going into their room and closing the door, but I can still hear them."

"I know what you mean. My parents always did that before they got divorced," Lydia said, looking sad herself.

"That's what I'm afraid of," Dory said, looking as if she were about to cry. "They keep saying everything will be okay, but it's not. Last night my dad left with a suitcase." Her voice grew angry. "I'm not supposed to fight with my brother. We're supposed to work our problems out and be nice to each other. Why is it okay for my parents to fight?"

"I don't know," Lydia said. "I thought it was my fault, but my mom told me she and my dad just couldn't get along with each other."

"What's it like now?" Dory asked, not really wanting to know. "I mean, do you ever see your dad?"

Lydia looked out the window as she answered. "I see him on most weekends. We have fun."

"I wish my parents would quit fighting and stay together," Dory said, wiping away a tear. "I'm scared."

I DON'T UNDERSTAND

Directions: Read each of the following questions. After each question, read the answers and circle one. You may circle more than one answer if you wish.

1. What is Dory really afraid of?
   a. She might be afraid she will not have enough food or a place to live if her parents get divorced.
   b. She might think she may have to move and leave her friends.
   c. She could be afraid that her mom and dad will stop loving her.
   d. She is worried that she might have to choose between her mom and her dad.

2. When the fighting begins between Dory's mother and father, whose fault is it?
   a. It could be her dad's fault.
   b. It could be her mom's fault.
   c. It could be Dory's fault.
   d. It could be both her mom's and her dad's fault, not Dory's.
   e. It could be nobody's fault. It just happens.

3. Why do parents get divorced?
   a. It happens because parents get tired of their kids.
   b. Parents get divorced because they are really mad at each other all the time.
   c. Nobody knows why.
   d. It happens when a dad and a mom can no longer work their problems out.

4. What can Dory do?
   a. She can understand that she didn't cause her parents to get divorced.
   b. Dory can tell God how she feels.
   c. She can let her parents worry about their relationship instead of worrying about it so much herself.
   d. Dory can realize that it is okay to feel lots of different things including sadness, fear, anger, hurt, and even nothing at all.

WHAT WOULD ISAIAH SAY?
ISAIAH 41:10

Isaiah was a prophet who wrote about God in the Old Testament. He lived at a time when God's people who lived in Israel were going through some rough times.

There were many things for God's people to fear, but God told Isaiah to tell the people that they need not be afraid or worried because God was on their side. God wanted to help them.

God gave this same advice to Abraham, the person in the Old Testament who started the nation of Israel. God said in Genesis, the first book of the Bible, that he would be with Abraham through difficult times (Genesis 15:1). God told people throughout the Bible that he wanted to be their friend. God has always wanted to help people through rough times. Sometimes people in the Bible believed God and sometimes they did not.

Let's pretend that Isaiah could talk to you today.

Isaiah wants to talk with kids whose parents have divorced or are divorcing. What do you think Isaiah might say to them?

55

I DON'T UNDERSTAND
TOPIC: PARENTAL DIVORCE

Group:_____

Date Used: _____

Purpose:
Divorce is a reality for many children today in a society where the divorce rate has leveled off at fifty percent. Children from divorced families need opportunities to talk with adults and their peers about their feelings. Kids not experiencing divorce can learn from and support their peers.

This Zinger works best in situations where all the kids have experienced divorce. It can also be used with kids and their divorced parents together. If you don't have parents with their children, provide the parents with a copy of the Zinger so they can talk with their kids later. If you use this Zinger with a group of kids who come from divorced and non-divorced families, you need to inform parents so that they can also process the experience with their kids.

Questions:
1. What is Dory really afraid of?
Use this question to let your kids talk about all of their fears. You can create a master list of fears on a chalkboard or newsprint for everyone to see. This shows your children that all their fears and worries are normal. They can see that other kids have felt the same things.

2. When the fighting begins between Dory's mother and father, whose fault is it?
Kids often blame themselves for their parents' troubled marriage or divorce. Use this question to emphasize the fact that kids are never at fault for their parents' marriage problems or divorce.

3. Why do parents get divorced?
Parents get divorced for many reasons, none of which are because of their kids. If kids have been told it was their fault, you can again emphasize that it is a parental problem. If parents blame kids for a divorce, those parents are not taking responsibility for their actions.

Your kids will list a number of reasons for divorce. You can tell them that God gives us the freedom to make choices. Sometimes parents make choices in life that are tough and not always wise. Getting divorced is never easy, but it does happen. Sometimes marriages last a lifetime. Sometimes marriages end in divorce.

4. What can Dory do?
Dory needs to know that she can't keep her parents' marriage together. She can learn to accept and adjust to what has happened. She can turn to God, sharing her feelings with him and understanding that he may not answer her prayers to keep her parents' marriage together.

Bible Story:
Kids should know that God may not give the answers they want to their prayers to save their parents' marriage or get their parents to marry again, but they can understand that God is available to listen to how they feel and be their friend.

God wants kids to come to him when they are feeling overburdened by their parents' problems (Matthew 11:28-30). God knows all about them, so they need not hide from him or feel guilty about what has happened to their families (Luke 12:7). God can give them the strength to go through the tough times a divorce creates (Philippians 4:13). God wants to be their friend (John 3:16).

Additional Scriptures: 2 Corinthians 1:3-4; Hebrews 13:5

ZINGER 11
WHO WILL KNOW?

"Come on, Greg. No one's going to know," Michael said as they walked to Michael's house after school.

"But I told my mom I'd be going to your house after school," Greg said.

Greg's mom and dad were both at work. His parents thought he was old enough to be by himself. They trusted him.

"Greg, there's nothing to do at my house. Let's go over to the pizza restaurant, play a few video games, and come straight back. Then you'll still be at my house like you told your mom. No problem," Michael said.

Greg thought about it. He didn't like lying to his parents. But he would be at Michael's house like he said. Just not all of the time. It would be fun to play video games. Besides, Michael was right. His parents would never find out.

WHO WILL KNOW?

Directions: Read each of the following questions. After each question, read the answers and circle one. You may circle more than one answer if you wish.

1. How is Greg not being honest with his mom by going to the pizza restaurant with Michael?
   a. Greg did not have permission to go to the pizza restaurant.
   b. Greg should tell his mom everything he does.
   c. Greg's mom would be worried if she tried to contact him and could not find him.
   d. His mom thinks he is at Michael's house.

2. What are some other ways kids are dishonest with their parents?
   a. Lying about getting homework done.
   b. Blaming something on someone else.
   c. Making an excuse for a big mistake.
   d. Watching TV shows they are not allowed to watch.

3. How would Greg's mom feel if she knew he had gone to the pizza restaurant?
   a. She would be sad.
   b. She would be really angry.
   c. She wouldn't care that much.
   d. She would feel hurt.

4. What else could Greg have done?
   a. There is nothing else he could have done.
   b. Greg could have suggested some fun activities that they could have done at Michael's house.
   c. Called his mom first to get permission.
   d. Told Michael he would go straight home if Michael kept pushing him to go play video games at the pizza restaurant.

MOMS AND DADS WANT HONEST KIDS
PROVERBS 22:6

Parents want their kids to be honest. They don't like it when their kids lie. Why is honesty so important to moms and dads? The Bible tells parents to work hard at raising their kids to do the right things so they will have good lives as kids and as adults. The book of Proverbs is full of good advice. The author tells parents to train their kids in the right way to live. If parents do this their children will know what is right and what is wrong when they grow up.

Honesty is one of the things God wants parents to teach their kids. Parents know honesty is important because they have watched many people get hurt by telling lies. Moms and dads know that honesty will keep their kids out of trouble.

Kids lie because they think lying will keep them out of trouble. But this is not true. When kids are not honest, they can get into even more trouble.

Telling the truth is sometimes hard to do. Kids lie to cover up their mistakes. They lie to be able to do things they aren't supposed to do. When kids lie they forget about what might happen to them if someone finds out about it. We call what happens the consequences. Kids also forget that lying to their parents breaks the trust their parents have in them.

Proverbs 12:5 says that kids who want to do the right thing will be honest, but kids who want to do the wrong thing will lie. Michael wanted to go play video games, but Greg did not have permission to go with him. That was wrong. He lied to Greg when he said Greg's parents would never find out. Greg was not being honest with his parents by going to the pizza restaurant.

Let's pretend that Greg's parents did find out that Greg went to play video games at the pizza restaurant. What are the consequences or all the things that could happen when Greg's parents find out that he was at the pizza restaurant instead of at Michael's house?

LEADER'S TIPS
WHO WILL KNOW?
TOPIC: HONESTY WITH PARENTS

Group: _____

Date Used: _____

Purpose:
Children at this age lie to cover up, manipulate, and protect themselves. Children's workers can help support parental training in honesty by encouraging kids to be honest with their parents. Use this Zinger to discuss the importance of honesty and the consequences of dishonesty with parents.

Questions:
1. How is Greg not being honest with his mom by going to the pizza restaurant with Michael?
Talk for a minute about what it means to be honest with parents. Let your group members provide reasons for their answers. This helps kids wrestle with the rules of honesty. Kids are egocentric and often consider just their perspective. This question can help your kids see how their actions can be either honest or dishonest in relationship to their parents.

2. What are some other ways kids are dishonest with their parents?
Ask your kids to add to this list. Many kids will want to tell stories about dishonesty. Use these stories as opportunities to clarify dishonesty and reinforce the need for honesty with parents.

3. How would Greg's mom feel if she knew he had gone to the pizza restaurant?
Kids need practice in taking others' viewpoints. This question can help kids understand how their actions affect their parents. Make a list of all the feelings parents might have when their kids are dishonest with them. Explore how these feelings affect parents.

4. What else could Greg have done?
It is important to explore with the kids ways they can do the right thing and keep their friends.

Bible Story:
This Bible story points out why parents want their kids to learn to be honest. God has instructed parents to train their kids and parents work hard at doing this.

One of the most important principles your group can learn from this story is that of consequences. God tells parents that the consequence of teaching kids about honesty and making right choices is better adult lives for their kids (Proverbs 22:6). The Fifth Commandment spells out a similar consequence when it says there is a promise of long life for honoring parents (Exodus 20:12). Your group needs to understand the consequences of lying and the effect it has on parent-child trust.

Additional Scriptures: Each of the following can be found in Proverbs. God likes honesty (11:1). Honesty guides the faithful while dishonesty is the guide that will destroy the unfaithful (11:3). Honesty will keep kids out of trouble in the long run but dishonest talk will get kids into trouble (12:13). A person's lies will one day be found out (12:19).

ZINGER 12
THE WAR IN CLASS

"I love free time," Selina said as she added another piece to her creation.

Selina and her friends Troy and Kevin were working together at the construction table. The other kids in their classroom were doing puzzles, reading, or painting.

Selina liked the construction table. There were hammers and screwdrivers, nails and screws, and pieces of wood to join together. Selina had decided to build a house.

"Bang, you're dead!"

Selina and Kevin jumped.

"Bang, you're dead," said Troy to Kevin pointing what looked like a toy gun at them. He had just finished building it.

"Troy, stop it," Selina said.

"Yeah, Troy, quit shooting us," Kevin said.

"What's going on here?" Mr. Carls asked. "Troy, you know we don't build weapons at the construction table!"

"I know, Mr. Carls, but I'm fighting a war," Troy said. "I need to shoot people to win."

"This sounds like something we might want to talk about as a class. Everyone sit down over on the carpet, please. Let's talk about war."

THE WAR IN CLASS

Directions: Read each of the following questions. After each question, read the answers and circle one. You may circle more than one answer if you wish.

1. Why do you think Troy wanted to play war in his classroom?
    a. Boys are supposed to fight in wars.
    b. Troy was a mean person.
    c. Troy watched lots of movies about war and wanted to act out what he saw in the movies.
    d. Playing war is fun.

2. Why did Mr. Carls think that war was an important topic for the class to discuss?
    a. He wanted the class to learn more about how to fight wars.
    b. He wanted to help answer kids' questions about war.
    c. He realized some kids might feel sad or hurt because of war.
    d. He thought people might be confused about war.

3. Why do you think countries go to war with each other?
    a. One country is mad at another country.
    b. Because wars are fun.
    c. A country wants to take things that don't belong to it from other countries.
    d. Mean people in charge of a country want to hurt people in other countries.

4. How do you think God feels about war?
    a. God likes countries to fight each other.
    b. God wants countries to work their problems out just like he wants us to work out our problems.
    c. God loves all people including the enemy in a war.
    d. God doesn't like war because people get hurt and killed.

BATTLES AND THE BIBLE
ISAIAH 2:4

There were lots of battles and wars described in the Bible. War is not new. God does not like war. But the Bible tells about wars from long ago because God wants us to know how he works in people's lives even during a war.

Jesus said that there would be wars and more wars (Matthew 24:6). But the Bible also promises us that there will be an end to war. Long ago, God told the prophet Isaiah that one day people would take all their weapons and turn them into farm tools. They would help instead of hurt people. People would no longer learn about war. Instead they would learn about peace. The Lord told Isaiah that nations would quit fighting each other. Can you imagine a time when people would not fight with each other? That's what God has promised for the future!

Today, Jesus Christ wants us to be peacemakers (Matthew 5:9). God wants us to work to help people get along. There are many ways you can be a peacemaker. You can pray for peace. You can find ways to get along with your brothers and sisters. When you are on the playground at school, you and your friends can help kids who want to fight work out their problems in other ways. You can solve problems in ways other than fighting.

Let's pretend that Isaiah could talk with your Sunday school class about war and peace. What questions would you ask the prophet Isaiah about war? What questions would you ask Isaiah about getting along with others?

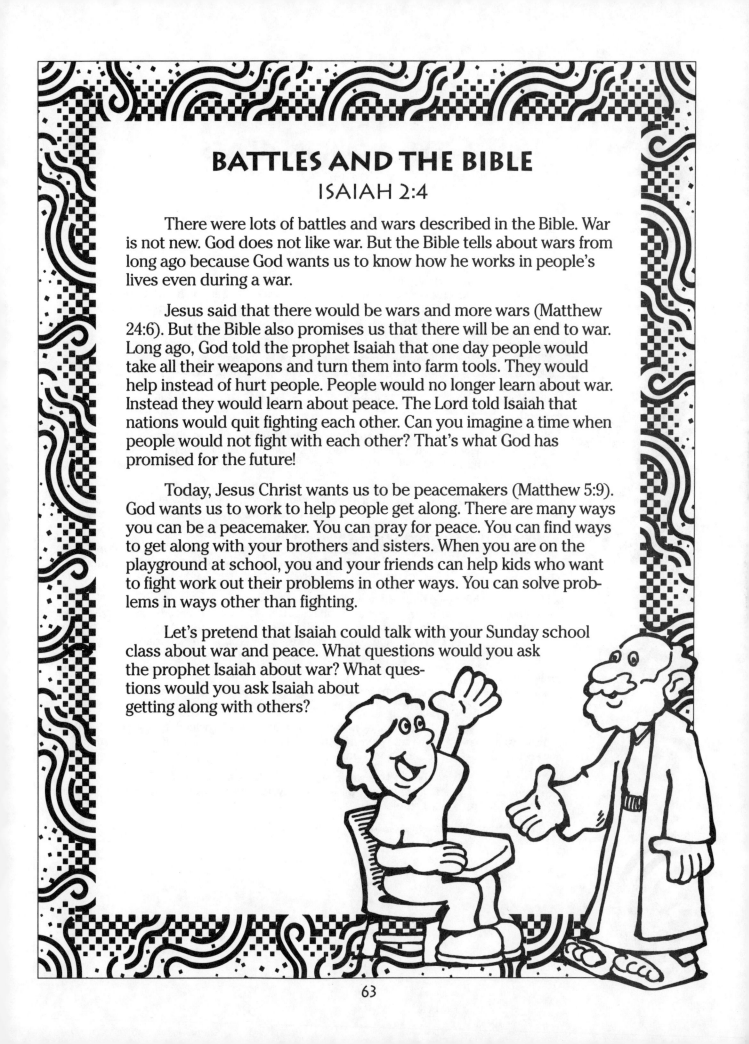

LEADER'S TIPS
THE WAR IN CLASS
TOPIC: WAR

Group: _____

Date Used: _____

Purpose:
There is a war going on right now somewhere in the world. Perhaps you are using this Zinger because the United States is involved in or affected by a specific war. Children have many questions about war and its effects. This Zinger can provide an opportunity to talk with kids about how Christians cope with war.

Questions:
1. Why do you think Troy wanted to play war in his school classroom?
Explore with your group why they think kids like to pretend war, play video war games, and watch war movies. At this age kids need to talk about the violence they see all around them. Kids are growing up in a culture that glorifies violence. Fighting is the way problems are resolved.

2. Why did Mr. Carls think war was an important topic for the class to discuss?
Talk with kids about the awfulness of war (don't use gory details; use general terms). Instead of glorifying the hurting and killing of others (even if it is pretend), Christians can be peacemakers.

If you are using this Zinger to talk about a specific war that is having an immediate impact on your kids, help the kids sort out the truth from the falsehoods they are hearing about the war.

3. Why do you think countries go to war with each other?
Point out that countries are made up of people. Countries fight for the same reasons people do. You can also talk with the kids about evil. Point out that some countries have evil leaders who can be very mean.

4. How do you think God feels about war?
Some kids may see God as strict and mean and responsible for war. Other kids may be mad at God because a parent was hurt in a war or is off fighting a war. Some kids will wonder why God lets wars happen. Use this opportunity to address your group's questions about God's attitude toward war.

Bible Story:
List all the questions your children have about war and peace. List them in two categories: international and personal. Then with the help of the class, answer the questions.

Point out to your group that there may be times when they have to defend themselves personally just as there may be times countries must defend themselves. But there is a difference between self-defense and aggression.

Spend some time talking about all the ways your kids can be peacemakers for Christ on an international level (letter writing to world leaders; prayers) and a personal level (getting along with siblings; conflict resolution).

Additional Scriptures: Psalm 20:7; John 14:27; Romans 12:18